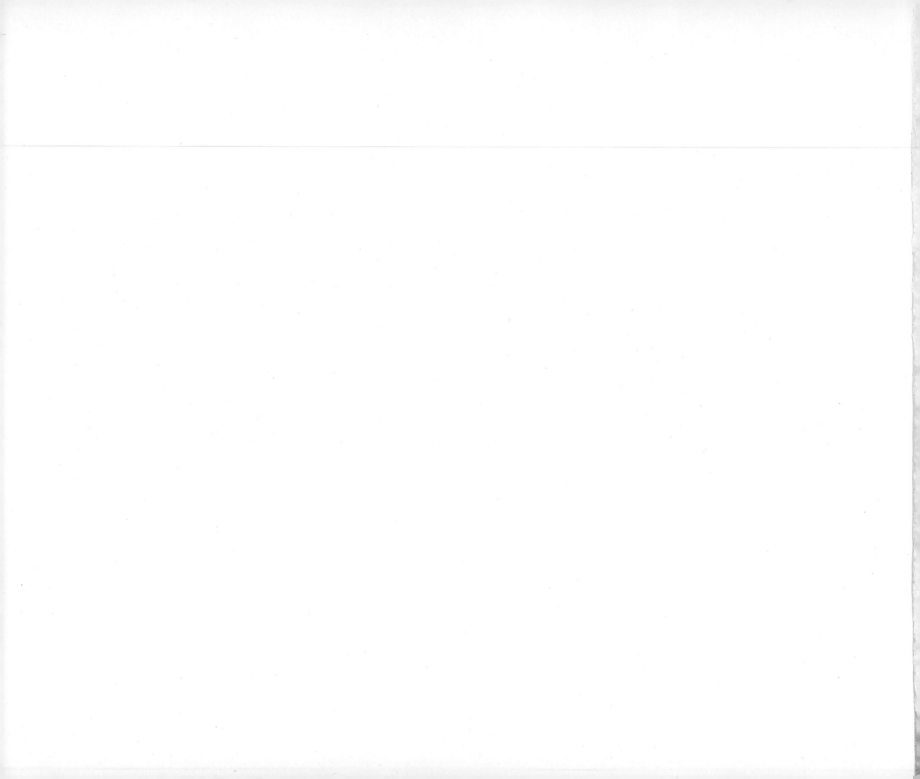

Under the Ice

Kids Can Press acknowledges the financial support of the Ontario Arts Council, the Canada Council
for the Arts and the Government of Canada, through the BPIDP, for our publishing activity.

Published in Canada by   Published in the U.S. by
Kids Can Press Ltd.   Kids Can Press Ltd.
29 Birch Avenue   2250 Military Road
Toronto, ON M4V 1E2   Tonawanda, NY 14150

www.kidscanpress.com

Written by Kathy Conlan, Louise Dickson, Iain Hunter
Edited by Valerie Wyatt and Charis Wahl
Designed by Julia Naimska
Printed and bound in Hong Kong, China, by Book Art Inc., Toronto

This book is smyth sewn casebound.

CM 02 0 9 8 7 6 5 4 3 2 1

National Library of Canada Cataloguing in Publication Data

Conlan, Kathleen Elizabeth, 1950–
        Under the ice

On cover: A Canadian Museum of Nature book.
ISBN 1-55337-001-5

1. Marine pollution — Polar Regions — Juvenile literature.
2. Marine biology — Polar regions — Juvenile literature.
3. Conlan, Kathy — Juvenile literature. 4. Marine biologists — Biography — Juvenile literature.
I. Dickson, Louise, 1959– II. Hunter, Iain
III. Title.

QH91.16.C65 2002   578.77'09163'2   C2001-904240-X

Kids Can Press is a *corus*™ Entertainment company

Under the Ice

Kathy Conlan

A Canadian Museum of Nature Book

Kids Can Press

Contents

My Dream

I am weightless, floating in a big empty room. Sea angels drift above me. Stars glimmer below. A chorus of wails, clicks and grunts spooks me, and I twist around to see the source of the sound. But there is nothing — nothing but a smooth, blue ceiling hung with crystal chandeliers.

This weird world is not a dream, but it is *my* dream. I am diving 30 m (100 ft.) down under the ice of Antarctica. The water is so cold that exposed flesh becomes numb in seconds, but my scuba gear protects me. I am free to enjoy the stunning beauty of the place.

I am a marine biologist and I'm studying the sea stars and other creatures that live on the sea bed. Although it can be cold and dangerous under the ice, this is my favorite place. I have been given a great gift — the opportunity to enter this vast ocean in order to learn how humans are affecting marine life in Antarctica.

I'm Kathy Conlan, the luckiest person in the world.

Dr. Kathy Conlan crouching in a cave sculpted out of an iceberg.

Sea stars and sea urchins slowly meander over the sea bed, and a "chandelier" of ice hangs down where salt has been squeezed out from the sea ice above.

A nudibranch glides over the sea bed. It is a kind of snail without a shell.

Call of the Deep

When I was a kid, I loved the outdoors. My family had a cottage and I spent most of the summer there swimming, sailing, making forts and climbing trees. I also went to summer camp. The lake was my kind of place, especially canoeing along the shore to surprise frogs and call the loons.

But it wasn't as if I knew, back then, what I wanted to be. At the end of high school, I had to decide. Because I loved the outdoors, I chose biology, the study of living things. Then, on a camping trip to Vancouver Island, I discovered the ocean.

I hold out a garter snake, rather gingerly, for my sisters Wendy (left) and Janet (right) to see.

Here I am at age two. Could you guess that I'd one day become a marine biologist?

Climbing around the rocks, I was fascinated by the stunning variety of life in the tide pools. Later I learned to scuba dive and discovered so much more. I was hooked! Marine biology was going to be my life, and I was going to study the creatures where they lived, in the ocean, not preserved in jars in the lab. So I went off to the University of Victoria to begin my studies. Along the way I married my university beau, Glenn, and, by the time I had finished my PhD in 1988, we had two small children.

My whole family, including our dog, Lochay, loved to camp.

My first job as a marine biologist was at the Canadian Museum of Nature. Then, in 1989, I got a taste of field research, and I loved it. To be a field biologist (a biologist who studies plants and animals where they are found), you have to be a certain type of person. You need to be an adventurer, love activity, put up with terrible weather conditions and the discomforts of camping — and take physical risks. And you have to do good science by setting up your experiments carefully and collecting data accurately, so your findings will give you the information you need.

The 1989 field trip happened when a team of researchers from Moss Landing Marine Laboratories in Monterey, California, asked me to join them studying sea otters in Alaska. It was a great opportunity and I jumped at it. The diving we did was amazing, and the next year led to an even bigger adventure. We all headed up to the Arctic to do some of the most challenging (and definitely the coldest) diving I had ever tried.

The tide pools on Vancouver Island blew me away. They were teeming with darting, colorful life.

Following the Icebergs

I sat on the edge of a small boat off the coast of Cornwallis Island, 1630 km (1013 mi.) inside the Arctic Circle, and stared at the ocean. The clouds loomed low and icy; the wind was raw. Ice floes and small icebergs lurked in the frigid gray water. Summer on the Arctic Ocean!

I was not looking forward to the cold, but my dive partners from Moss Landing, John Oliver and Hunter Lenihan, were already in the water and I was eager to join them. I wanted to see the ice scours. These scars in the sea floor are caused as enormous chunks of ice scrape the bottom, digging up the sea bed and squashing the sea creatures that live on it. It was the scours that John and Hunter had been studying. Now it was my turn to see one.

Here I'm about to roll backward into the arctic water. Stewart Lamerdin is the dive tender, checking gear and making sure the way is clear.

A scour can be wider than a 12-lane highway, with walls of sediment several meters (yards) high on either side. The Arctic coasts are littered with them. In fact, from underwater, the sea bed looks like a badly plowed field, torn up every which way. We wanted to find out how the scours had affected life on the sea bed. Did the animals come back after the ice had gone through, or did the scours do permanent damage?

Ice Scours

Ice scours destroy, but they also make new life possible. The ice gouges out fresh, rich sea bed, which stimulates the growth of bacteria and tiny plants called diatoms. This attracts all sorts of creatures, some drawn to the wealth of food, others to an open space where there are few predators. So the sea floor becomes a parade in slow motion, with new animals coming and others slowly moving on to new scours. It may take more than 50 years for a community to return and many hundreds of years for all trace of the ice scour to disappear. Where the sea bed is protected from ice scouring, marine life is not as diverse. So ice scours are a good thing — as long as they don't happen too often.

I perched precariously under the weight of my dive tank and weight belt, grasped my mask and flipped backward into the coldest water I'd ever been in. As I surfaced, I grabbed for the ropes that ran along the sides of our inflatable boat. The current was strong, and I didn't want to be swept away.

Currents aren't the only hazard of arctic diving. Drifting ice can overturn a boat or crush a diver who doesn't move out of the way fast enough. It can even cut off a diver's route to open water — and air.

The dive was worth the risks — more than worth them. We sank slowly through the water, showing each other little jellyfish and copepods as they darted out of our way. Suddenly the sea bed rose out of the green depths, and we saw our first scour, a ghostly white gouge in a bed of pink-coated rock.

Surrounding the scours were massive kelps sheltering small shrimps and providing food for snails to graze on. Pink, red and cream sea anemones clustered like bouquets of flowers. Brittle stars, sea cucumbers, sea urchins and delicate soft corals covered the sea bed. What seemed to be a small purple bush turned out to be an isopod, with babies hanging off her antennae. Sea spiders, some the size of my hand, moved ponderously among the rocks, hunting for coral. Arctic cod peeked out warily from among the kelp.

I took this picture of my friend Jonna Engel diving in kelp. I was amazed to see such lush plants underwater. The kelp capture the Sun's energy during the long days in summer and grow in winter.

Arctic cod are essential food for seals and whales. Once I saw a huge school of arctic cod that narwhals and belugas had corralled into a bay. The whales kept them there for three days, providing a great feast for themselves, as well as seals and seabirds.

Underwater — and above water — the Arctic is a photographer's dream. So over the next few weeks, between working dives, I took my camera along and snapped these pictures. I wanted to remember the beauty of the place and the people I met.

Getting to know some of the Inuit kids from Resolute Bay (Qausuittuq) was especially fun. They were curious about our gear, so we invited them to try it on. The most common comment was "Boy, is this stuff heavy." Of course, once you're in the water, you don't feel the weight.

This nudibranch eats anemones and soft corals and stores their microscopic harpoons in its "branches." When threatened, it will fire off these "stolen" harpoons to defend itself.

We brought our gear along when we were invited to Qarmartalik school in Resolute Bay. The kids knew about our ice scour study because **some of their relatives were working with us. In Resolute Bay, everyone knows everyone.**

This lobster relative is called *Arcturus baffini*. The female boosts her young up into the water on her long antennae so they can catch food passing by in the current.

Our research showed that ice scours *do* affect the animals on the sea bed. However, these are natural changes and the sea life is able to recover. But what about changes caused by people? What, for instance, would pollution do to the sea bed? It seemed I was going find out. My California friends invited me to study the impact of human pollution the following year. But not in the Arctic. Instead, we would be flying to within a few hundred kilometers (miles) of the South Pole. I was going to Antarctica to dive under the ice.

When sea ice drifts ashore, we can't reach our dive sites. Then we take time to soak up the beautiful arctic atmosphere. Bob Harmes and my daughter Janelle are mirrored in the still waters of an arctic August night.

Getting There

Ottawa to Los Angeles to Christchurch, New Zealand. Nearly 15 000 km (9300 mi.) in 27 hours, and only then does the real journey to Antarctica begin. We were heading for the United States's McMurdo Station, the largest science base in Antarctica. The final leg of the flight from Christchurch would take another eight hours.

I had spent weeks preparing for my three-month stint in Antarctica. Unpredictable antarctic weather makes emergency medical fly-ins dangerous — for pilots and doctors, as well as patients. So I had thorough medical and dental examinations before I left home.

I had shipped most of my science supplies, but I still had a mountain of dive, collecting and camera gear to pack. Then there were the permits. Scientists need permits to run experiments in Antarctica and permits to take collections back home when they leave.

In New Zealand, we were outfitted in antarctic gear and put through an orientation course. We were told always to carry emergency provisions. We also learned to recognize signs of hypothermia (very low body temperature), because when you're caught in a blizzard away from the base, there's nowhere

The plane to Antarctica is a tight fit. You have to squeeze your knees between the person's knees across from you. If the weather turns bad at McMurdo, you might get almost there, only to have to turn back.

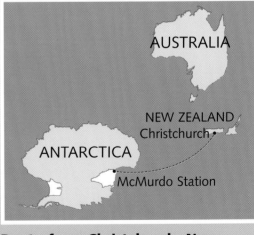

Route from Christchurch, New Zealand, to McMurdo station, Antarctica

to warm up. And although we were going to one of the coldest places on Earth — hardly a beach holiday — we were instructed to always wear sunscreen and sunglasses to protect us against UV radiation and snow blindness.

Waiting to fly became a guessing game. It all depended on the weather at McMurdo. Up before dawn, we would bundle in our winter gear and wait for hours for our boarding call, sweating in the balmy New Zealand morning. Sometimes we would get the signal to go. More often, we would be turned away and told to return the same time the next day.

It was a relief to finally board the military Hercules propeller plane. Nearly 60 scientists and support staff were crammed into rows of cot-shaped seats. Once underway, people could get up and sprawl on the piles of cargo to stretch their legs. The noise of the engines was so loud that trying to talk was useless, so we took turns peeking out the small windows.

When my turn came, I looked out and saw huge icebergs locked in the sea ice. As we got closer, I could see the Transantarctic Mountains that stretch across Antarctica. Through the valleys flowed glaciers — rivers of ice — their edges wrinkled and cracked where they rubbed against the rock.

At last the plane's skis bumped onto the runway of ice and we taxied to a halt. The doors opened, and I felt an icy blast of antarctic air. My heart pounded with excitement. Wobbling on cramped legs, I squinted in the sudden glare of the sun off the stark, white ice. Then it hit me — I was actually in Antarctica.

The pilot invited me up front. When I looked out I saw mountains, glaciers, and the icebergs above, which looked like an arrow pointing the way to Antarctica.

Frozen Continent

Eighteen countries have 37 research stations operating year-round in Antarctica and more that are seasonal. This is the U.S. McMurdo Station, the largest of them all. It's home to about 1200 in summer and 200 in winter.

When I landed in Antarctica that first time, in November 1991, spring was turning into summer. (Because Antarctica is in the southern hemisphere, its seasons are the reverse of what I was used to in Canada.) It certainly didn't feel summery — the temperature was a cool –10°C (14°F) and there was snow everywhere.

Antarctica is the coldest, windiest, driest continent on Earth. In fact, it is considered a polar desert. It is about 14 million square kilometers (about 5 million square miles) in area — twice the size of Australia — and 98 per cent of it is covered with ice.

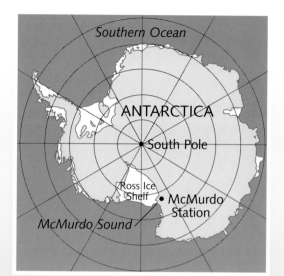

Winds often sweep across the plateau where the South Pole is located, dropping the temperature to as low as –97°C (–143°F), cold enough to freeze skin in seconds. No wonder people who come to work here call themselves the Frozen Chosen. And now I was going to be one of them.

We headed to the waiting bus that would take us to McMurdo Station, or Mactown, as it is called. A 2 m (6 ft.) layer of ice was all that separated us from the ocean beneath. Before long I would be diving under it to see the sea creatures below. It was a thrilling and slightly scary thought.

There was no time to dawdle. We were hustled into the bus, and it rolled ponderously over the frozen McMurdo Sound toward our new home, Mactown.

When I first stepped off the plane, I was all buttoned and zipped up. But I soon learned to let my jacket flap open. It's considered cooler — in all senses of the word.

Exploring Antarctica

I was one of a long line of visitors to Antarctica. The earliest visitors were sealers, whalers and explorers.

Explorer James Clark Ross of Britain sailed into McMurdo Sound in 1841. He named the two nearby volcanoes after his two ships, the *Erebus* and the *Terror*. Robert Falcon Scott of Britain arrived in January 1902. His ship, *Discovery*, was his base for exploring and conducting scientific research. Ernest Shackleton, who had been a member of Scott's expedition, returned on the *Nimrod* in 1908 to Cape Royds. Members of his party climbed Mount Erebus and reached the magnetic South Pole.

The bones of Scott's sled dogs can still be seen at his base camp.

Scott returned in 1911 and reached the South Pole in January the following year. But a month earlier, a team led by the Norwegian Roald Amundsen had reached the Pole first. Scott and his four companions froze to death trying to get back to their base camp.

In 1914, Sir Ernest Shackleton planned to cross the continent, but before he could land, his ship, *Endurance*, was crushed in the ice and sank. After 22 months, Shackleton and a small band of men found help after crossing 1300 km (800 mi.) of open sea in a small boat. They returned to Antarctica to save the rest of the crew. Not a single life was lost.

Inside Scott's base camp everything looked as it did 90 years ago, when he left it for the last time.

Visiting explorer Robert Scott's base camp at Cape Evans was an eerie experience. Scott and four others did not make it back to this camp after they reached the South Pole in 1912.

On Station

As we drove into Mactown, I felt like a kid going to a new school for the first time. I was excited, but nervous, too. What would the diving be like? Would my work go well? Would I fit in?

Mactown isn't much to look at on the outside, but inside it is a fascinating place full of atmosphere and interesting people.

Believe it or not, this photo of the dorms was taken late at night. I was struck by the appearance of the full moon, which I had watched over the days waxing from left to right — backward to my northern eyes.

Learning the ropes started on day one. We were shown where we'd eat and sleep. In the galley, we would be fed like royalty. There'd be three big meals a day, plus loads of chocolate bars and snacks in between. But we would need it. Diving and hauling heavy equipment around in the cold is hard work.

Beakers, as we scientists were dubbed, got the best dorms. We were two to a room, sharing a toilet and shower. Downstairs was the common room, with a TV, pool table and sauna. We could rent skis or musical instruments, go bowling, work out in the weight room, or play volleyball or basketball. Mactown even has its own TV and radio stations and a newspaper.

On that first day, we were told how to sort garbage: food scrapings in one place, batteries in another, empty plastic bottles in a third. We learned that the main routes out from the station are marked by flags on bamboo poles. Red and green flags mean the route is safe. Black flags mean danger — spreading cracks, dive holes or thinning ice.

The next day, storms were on the agenda. Before newcomers were allowed to go anywhere, we had to learn how to deal with nasty weather. There were strict rules, and nobody had permission to break them. Ever.

Storms can come up suddenly. So, rule number one was: never leave the base without shelter and five days of emergency rations, and always let people know where you're going and for how long. (If you're an hour overdue, the search and rescue team is sent out, and they can get very crabby if they're called out in brutal weather because you've forgotten to call in.)

By the end of our orientation, we knew the ropes — and the rules. Now it was time to go to work.

A Blanket of Snow

In case a storm comes up when we are away from the station, newcomers are shown how to build an emergency shelter called a "quinzee." First you build a small raised base of snow. Then you pile your sleeping bags in a mound in the middle and pack layers of snow over them, leaving a smallish hole on one side. Pull the bags out through the hole, and you've made a cave. It's small, but it's bright, and the snow will insulate you from the cold.

Later, when I returned home, I showed my son Michael how to build a quinzee (above).

On the Ice

Going to work, if you're a marine biologist in Antarctica, isn't just a matter of getting dressed, hopping into the car and heading to a nice warm office. You bundle up, drive out across the ice in a tractored vehicle called a Spryte, suit up in about 25 kg (55 lb.) of scuba gear, pick open your dive hole, and lower yourself into water so cold your equipment might freeze.

The morning of my first dive my stomach was churning. I was scared — no, I was terrified. But I also felt so privileged to be going — and I was determined not to let the rest of the team see my fear.

Getting through ice 2 m (6 ft.) thick is no mean feat. First a bulldozer clears the snow, then a huge auger drills the 1.5 m (5 ft.) wide hole. Actually, two holes, just in case a diver gets into trouble and can't make it back to the entry hole.

Marc Slattery and Dan Bockus help me suit up. Marc is attaching my mitts to rings that will keep the water out. This "dry" system prevents hands from freezing — unless a glove is punctured.

We hauled our equipment into a dive hut that had been dragged over the hole. It had a stove to keep us warm, lots of drinking water and chocolate bars to fuel up on between dives. A trap door in the floor opened to the dive hole.

The routine of suiting up kept me focused for a while. Over my long underwear and bunny suit, I was wearing a rubber-coated canvas dry suit. It had built-in boots and latex seals at the neck and wrists to keep the water out. I attached my backpack to my special, twin-valved tank and screwed a breathing regulator to each valve. The regulators are important. They reduce the high-pressure air in the tanks so the diver's lungs don't get damaged. You have two separately attached regulators, so there's a spare in case the first one freezes.

The dive hut is our home away from home when we are diving. Parked beside it is our Spryte. The Spryte won't set any speed records, but it can handle the ice conditions.

I sat down at the edge of the dive hole and put on my fins, ankle weights and dive knife; tightened the dive computer on my wrist; pulled on my mitts and buckled on my 17 kg (37 lb.) weight belt. I spit into my mask and rubbed the saliva on the glass to keep it from fogging up while I was diving, washed it out, then slipped it on.

The dive tender helped me strap the tanks to my back and attach the air hose to my suit. I checked my tank pressure to be sure that the air valve was open. I clamped my teeth around the mouthpiece of the regulator. Then, like a fat, apprehensive seal, I looked down into the black dive hole.

Hole? This wasn't a hole — I was looking down a 2 m (6 ft.) tunnel of ice!

Letting Go

"Kathy! You're next!" The most exciting and terrifying words I've ever heard.

I was sitting on the floor of the dive hut with my legs dangling into the tunnel of ice. I could see water below me. It was black and it looked cold. The moment had come. I took a deep breath, held on to my mask and pushed off.

Splash! I was in the water. I bobbed for a minute, catching my breath — and my thoughts. "Okay. This is it. You've come this far, so do it!" And then I let some air out of my suit and began to descend.

The cold enveloped my face like a mask and my lips became numb. I could hear the blood pounding in my head and my breath rasping through my regulator. Silver air bubbles fizzed upward as I pushed with hands and knees to

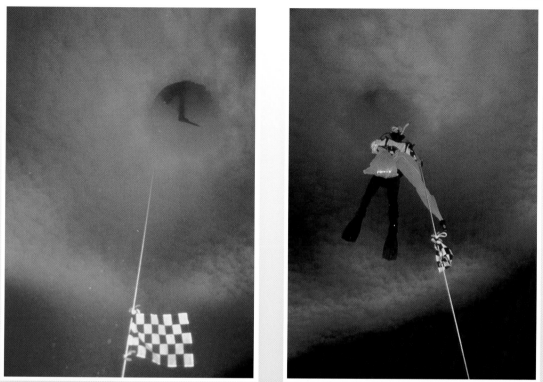

I emerged from the tunnel feet first, grasping the dive line. The flag signals where the hole is and which way the current is running. Notice my snorkel? Nobody wears a snorkel under the ice because it's useless there. Wearing one was like a neon sign flashing "first timer."

ease myself down the ice tunnel. I kept a death grip on the dive line — my link to the surface.

Suddenly I panicked — I couldn't feel the regulator. Was it still in place? Had I lost it? I was so frightened I forgot that it's too big to fall out of my mouth. Then my brain took over. "Hey, Kathy," I told myself. "You're still breathing, aren't you? So it's got to be there, right?" Right. The tunnel ended and I was under the ice.

I floated like a skydiver over the gently sloping ocean floor. The ice above me was like a smooth, white sky. The dive hole glowed like a moon, and the cracks in the ice were neon blue, like flashes of lightning. I saw tread marks left by tractors and the comforting shadow of the dive hut.

No question about it: I was a guest in one of the most hard-to-reach places on Earth.

Antarctic Gallery

Once under the ice, you can see all the way down to the sea bed. After the long winter, there is barely anything in the water to cloud your view. As in the Arctic, I was amazed at the color and diversity of marine life.

Underwater you have to be quick to get photos of fast-moving fish and seals. Sea bed creatures are more co-operative — most move slowly or not at all, giving you lots of time to compose a picture.

Antarctica holds a special attraction for underwater photographers. The Southern Ocean that circles it has been cold far longer than the Arctic Ocean, so there has been more time for uniquely polar species to evolve. In the Arctic, the ocean receives a good supply of marine immigrants from the Pacific and Atlantic Oceans, but the Antarctic Circumpolar Current acts as a barrier to all but the strongest swimmers. Because of this, the Southern Ocean has an amazing array of species not found anywhere else.

These photos show some of the animals I encountered on the sea bed along the coast of McMurdo Sound. They are not isolated species, as they appear here, but part of a community that lives together. Most of their activity occurs over eating — or attempting to avoid being eaten.

Desmonema is a jellyfish the size of a basketball that drifts under the ice hunting for small animals, which it captures with its long tentacles.

When the sun gets strong in the summer and ice begins to melt, the water fills up with tiny, drifting plants and animals called plankton. The largest of the animals you see here would be about the size of this "O."

These fan worms spread their fans to catch whatever drifts by. If they sense danger, they pull back into their tubes in a flash. To avoid startling them so that I could get this picture, I had to drift by, hardly moving.

Sometimes there are so many sea stars and sea urchins that the bottom looks like a dance floor crowded with flamenco dancers in red dresses. As long as the big, white sea star is healthy, it will be safe among them. If it is hurt, the red sea stars will attack.

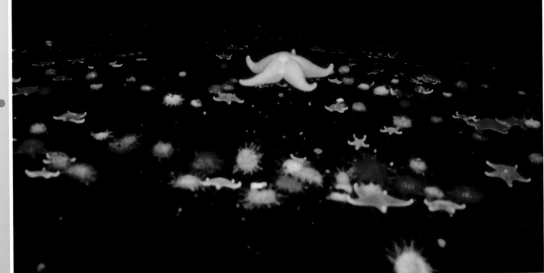

These two sea anemones have captured a jellyfish (in pink between them). They kill their prey with tiny harpoon-like spears in their tentacles.

Volcano sponges can grow larger than humans. These ones are probably several centuries old. Sponges suck in water through little holes on their surface and filter out bits of food. Then they spit out the water through a central hole.

These sea cucumbers are related to sea stars and sea urchins.

Ribbon worms will eat almost anything on the sea bed. Once I put out leftover spareribs. The worms ate them whole. Their bodies distended into rectangles around the ribs.

The animals (yes, they are animals) in the foreground are capturing whatever food drifts by in the water. That's a lot of mouths to feed.

This spiky hot dog is actually a worm crawling along the sea bed. It slurps up mud and eats any bits of food it contains. Usually this kind of animal is smaller than my thumbnail, but in Antarctica, it's nearly as long as my hand.

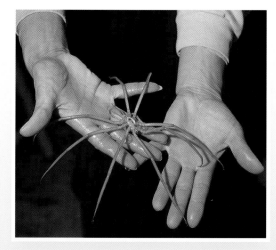

My friend Stacy holds one of the sea spiders that roam ponderously over the sea bed, eating soft corals. The males carry around their youngsters on their backs.

This antarctic toothfish can live for up to 45 years. Although it lives 500 m (1640 ft.) below the surface, it is being fished and sold as Chilean sea bass. It may one day become extinct, unless something is done to preserve it.

On the Bottom

As a scientist, I have to look at things closely — first impressions can be deceiving. And Antarctica is no exception. It's beautiful, for sure; but it's the not-so-beautiful effects — the pollution — that I would be studying.

Until recently, visitors simply dumped their garbage in Antarctica. You can still see crates, barrel hoops and jars from Scott's and Shackleton's expeditions, and even the skeletons of some of their sled dogs. Later visitors burned what they could and created a dump for much of the rest. But the garbage released harmful chemicals.

This closeup of the Corn Pile at the end of the sewage pipe gives you some idea of what we found. Can you see anything familiar?

The McMurdo sewage pipe spews ground-up kitchen waste, gray water and human waste into the ocean. The white coating is actually millions of bacteria feeding on the waste.

We found this old tractor sitting near the sewage pipe. It was probably abandoned out on the ice and fell through.

At the 1996 Halloween dance at McMurdo, Jonna Engel and I dressed up as Corn Pile Queens, wearing dresses covered with yellow plastic and stuff from the garbage bins.

At McMurdo, there was another problem. The military had abandoned its old equipment on the sea ice. But the ice didn't support it for long. Now tractors, hoses and pieces of aircraft litter the sea bed where they fell through. Even worse are the barrels that have leaked their waste and contaminated the ocean floor.

Today, garbage is shipped back to Washington state, where most of it can be recycled. Well, not all of it is shipped back — human waste and gray water (water from cooking and bathing) are ground up and pumped into the sea through a waste pipe. This is where the science came in. I was to be part of a team that was trying to figure out where the human waste ended up and what effect it had on the animals that live on the sea bed.

We could track the lighter bits of waste. They spew out of the waste pipe and rise to the undersurface of the ice. Currents push them along the shore for as much as a kilometer (over half a mile). The heavier waste settles on the sea bed at the end of the pipe.

We collected different kinds of sea bed animals and examined them in the lab. We found evidence that some of them had taken human waste, and therefore human bacteria, into their bodies. Even some of the seals seemed to have human bacteria in their bodies.

The news wasn't good. Human waste is harming the rich community that lives on the sea bed. A few hardy types flourish, but most don't, and the diversity of the sea life is being destroyed.

Working at the end of the waste pipe was no picnic. Because corn doesn't get ground up and accumulates at the end of the pipe, the area was nicknamed the Corn Pile. Our team soon got the reputation of being the dirtiest, smelliest, grossest science group at the station.

Underwater Science

In 1997, I was invited to be part of a team that would do an experiment on the sea bed. We wanted to know whether different sorts of animals were affected by different kinds of pollution.

The plan was to dig up clean sediment from the sea bed and pollute it. In some dishes of sediment, we'd mix in vegetables from the kitchen to mimic waste coming from the sewage pipe. Others would get copper, a sample of the material the military dumped. Then we'd dig these dishes of polluted sediments (and some without any garbage) back into the sea bed. A year later, we'd collect the dishes to see which animals had colonized them. Sounds easy, but it wasn't.

Digging up dirt underwater is tricky. I'd hover close to the bottom, scoop up some sediment, then dump it into a bucket — and watch half of it swirl back out and drift away. Once a bucket was full, I'd haul it over to a line and clip it on so that it could be pulled to the surface. Swimming with a heavy bucket of mud was a challenge. I did a sideways crab walk, half lifting, half dragging the bucket. I was panting with exhaustion and had to keep a close eye on my air supply to make sure I didn't run out far away from the dive hole.

In all, it took us about 80 dives to dig 560 dishes into the sea bed at different sites. Why so many? Scientists do not jump to conclusions based on a small sample, because the results might be due to chance. So we set out a large sample in various locations to make sure that any trends we spotted really were trends.

We dug our dishes of sediment into the sea bed and waited to see what would be attracted to them.

Sea stars are great scavengers. These are eating a jellyfish that swam too close to the bottom and got stuck.

We thought we were all set for a year's wait to see what settled in, but we were in for a surprise. We discovered that the big roving animals — urchins, ribbon worms and especially sea stars — loved the vegetable mix. They swarmed our dishes, and we were afraid there would be nothing left for the little guys.

Our solution was to put up a 2 m (6 ft.) high fence. Try pounding stakes and tying up fencing underwater! Everything works in slow motion. And worse, the sharp fencing punctured our dive gloves, giving us excruciating cold water soakers. It took weeks of hard work to put up that fence, but it didn't stop the sea stars. They just went over the top, like pirates swarming a treasure ship. To keep them out, we finally had to put a cage over each dish.

The next year, we were eager to find out what had happened. We geared up and headed underwater. Everything looked just as we had left it. We collected the samples and headed back to the lab. Our vegetable mix smelled of rotten eggs, but it was teaming with sewage worms, even though McMurdo's waste pipe was 10 km (6 mi.) away. Our copper mix, on the other hand, held lots of shrimp-like animals.

So, as we had suspected, different animals were drawn to different kinds of pollution. We hope that this information will help scientists studying ocean pollution in the future. For example, if scientists were to notice an overabundance of sewage worms, our research would tell them to be on the lookout for organic pollution nearby. In effect, the animals would act as "indicators" of certain types of pollution.

Hunter Lenihan, Stacy Kim, Christian McDonald, Jon Grabowski and I would sieve sea-bed samples for hours, cracking jokes all the while. Hunter gave everyone a nickname. Mine was "Captain Chaos," coined after a particularly disorganized field trip we had together in the Arctic.

Look at all the sea stars and urchins climbing our fence!

Danger Under the Ice

When you're diving under the ice, you have to keep track of how your equipment is doing and where the dive hole is. Otherwise, you can find yourself in trouble, as I learned during my first season in Antarctica.

I'd made a few dives and was just starting to get comfortable when it happened. Equipment failure — every diver's nightmare. It was a dark dive and I was down deep. Suddenly it became hard to breathe and then, strangely, too easy. Something was wrong. *Whoosh!* I was surrounded by a rush of bubbles. My regulator had frozen open. My air supply was pouring out into the ocean.

I had been swimming with my buddies from one dive hole to another, but I was behind the others. Where was the dive line? It was too dark to see it. I wanted to call out, but of course, no one could hear me.

Nitrogen poisoning

Making repeated dives, as we did while setting up our experiment on the sea bed, puts divers at risk of nitrogen poisoning. Nitrogen can build up in your body and make you dopey. Your brain goes stupid and slow, and you can't focus to make quick, life-saving decisions. To prevent nitrogen narcosis (poisoning), we use personal dive computers, which monitor our dive time, depth and rate of ascent so that we can gauge how much nitrogen is in our tissues. The danger of narcosis is one important reason for diving with a buddy. If you're "narced," your partner should notice your weird behavior and get you to the surface.

Now, with my air gushing out around me, I swam frantically to catch up. It seemed like an eternity. My legs began to cramp with the effort. Then, in the distance, I saw it — the dive line and checkered flags of the second hole. All I wanted to do was get out fast, but I knew that surfacing too fast can be just as dangerous as running out of air. You risk a deadly embolism (a gas bubble in your body that halts blood flow). I forced myself to go slowly and reached the surface just as the last bit of air ran out of the tank.

It was only when I had calmed down in the dive hut that I remembered what I should have known underwater — all divers carry a second regulator. If I hadn't panicked, I could have signaled to one of the other divers to switch my remaining air supply to my other regulator and come up more slowly. My panic had put me in unnecessary danger.

We do everything possible to dive safely, but the cold and dark under the ice can pose unexpected risks. I learned never to forget that under the ice is a hostile environment for humans.

Sealing Friendships

One day, I was working away on the sea bed when I felt a tug on my fin. I looked around into the puppy face of a Weddell seal. Adult seals usually stay away from people underwater, but this one was a youngster who hadn't yet learned to be cautious.

I had the feeling I was being checked out as a possible playmate. The seal rested its head in the cup of my outstretched hand — almost as if it were sniffing. I rubbed my hand down its body as it drifted by. Then it rolled over on its back, did a graceful somersault and reached for my fin again.

Watching a seal underwater is a treat. It does an aquatic ballet that makes human divers feel awkward by comparison.

A young seal waits for its mother
to return. Behind it, the ice from a
glacier rears up into frozen pinnacles
when it runs into the sea ice.

Our research aims at protecting all the animals of Antarctica, but I have to admit it: some are just more fun than others.

When we dive, we can hear the Weddell seals calling to one another in a weird assortment of siren-like calls, whines, deep grunts and clicks that sound like a motorboat slowing down and cutting its engine. The males get pretty aggressive during the mating season in late November and vocalize to scare off intruders in their territories.

The females give birth to their pups on the ice the following October. The newborns look like little dolls wrapped in huge sleeping bags. Their mother's rich milk fattens them up quickly, though, and in six weeks they've grown into their skin and are ready for their first swim in the ocean.

Once I got to share my dive hole with a young seal. He was being picked on by a big male and trying to get away. As I was swimming up the ice tunnel to

the surface, I felt this young seal butt me in … well … the butt. Then he surfaced beside me, and we were nose to nose, as if he was about to give me a kiss.

Luckily, I had reached the dive hole first. Otherwise, I would have had to wait until he decided to leave, which might have been some time if the big guy stayed around. And if he hadn't found my dive hole? Weddell seals make their own by scraping away the ice with their teeth.

It's illegal to approach wildlife in Antarctica. But sometimes, if you stay really still and are really patient, they will come to you.

Seals

Weddell seals, like the one you see here, were hunted for food by early explorers. Other seals were hunted for their fur. So many fur seals were taken that they came close to extinction in Antarctica. Their fur was made into felt hats and long coats. Seal oil lit the lamps of Europe before petroleum-based oils became available. Today, antarctic seals are protected, and their numbers are increasing. Still, it's a rare thrill to swim with one.

Penguins

One morning we were making our way over the ice to go for a dive when we were greeted by a penguin, who casually shuffled up to us. Now, everyone thinks of penguins and the Antarctic together. But penguins are usually found near open water, and McMurdo Station is locked in by sea ice until late in the summer.

I wondered if maybe we should do something, but the old hands paid no attention. "Forget it," one said. "Every so often one gets lost. But it finds its way back home in a day or two."

I pictured a regular stream of penguin visitors, but, in fact, we had to travel to the Adélie colony at Cape Royds to see penguins in any numbers. Several thousand Adélie penguins swim south to breed there. They sit on their eggs or add to their nests of stones by snatching stones from other nests, like shoppers at a Boxing Day sale.

This fat, fuzzy and pigeon-toed Adélie youngster will soon grow a swimsuit of waterproof feathers. While in the ocean, it will clamber onto drift ice and use it as a raft to escape hungry leopard seals and orca whales.

These Adélies guard their stone nests — and steal others' stones if they can.

Out on the sea ice, close to open water, are the Emperors, the largest of the penguins. They stand up to 112 cm (44 in.) high, about a third taller than the Adélies.

The female lays a single egg in the winter and passes it over to her partner. The male holds it on his feet to keep it off the ice, covering it with a flap of skin for warmth. The males huddle together to keep warm in the punishing antarctic winter. In July, the coldest part of the winter, the chicks hatch, just as their mothers are returning from feeding in open water many hundreds of kilometers (miles) away. The males haven't eaten in four months, and they are thin and hungry. They pass the chicks back to the females and head to open water to fatten up and return with more food.

These Emperor penguins did not seem to mind my taking a plankton sample from their dive hole. Around McMurdo the plankton lack krill, the penguins' main food, so the penguins have to dive deeper for fish and squid.

For a moment there is some confusion about who is taking the photograph — me or the penguins.

On land, the Emperors are comical. You find them standing chest to chest, trumpeting. Their usual motion is a clumsy waddling. If they want to move fast, they toboggan on their tummies, paddling with their flippers and feet. But seeing them underwater, I was in awe of their speed and agility. They can dive to 300 m (1000 ft.) for 10 minutes at a time, hunting for fish and squid.

It's amazing to watch the Emperors jetting in groups toward the surface in a shower of silver bubbles. The bubbles are air released from under their feathers. Scientists think the streams of bubbles help the penguins hide from leopard seals and orca whales. Whatever the reason, it makes a spectacular underwater show for divers.

One day, we saw a group of Emperors in the distance. We got out of our Spryte and sat down to see if curiosity would draw them over. Sure enough, they filed up, stopped in line before us, and arched their heads first to the right, then to the left, in unison, as if to greet us.

Under the Midnight Sun

When we arrive in early October, the sun is still low in the evening, staining the mountains and sea ice pink. By late October, the sun never sets and we live under a midnight sun that will last until late February.

The perpetual daylight scrambles your body clock. I might eat dinner at midnight, go to bed at 2:00 A.M. or later, then get up at 10:00 A.M.. The days are filled with diving and work in the lab. But even scientists need to play. Whenever we had free time, a group of us would head out.

Away from Mactown, there's a wonderful feeling of space and freedom. You can see for miles, and there's nothing but mountains and ice.

You can feel very small in Antarctica, especially when you come up against a huge chunk of ice like this one. It has broken off an ice shelf and is called a "tabular berg."

It was after midnight when I took this picture of our tents, looking like a group of sleeping turtles, on the sea ice in Granite Harbor.

On one outing, I walked the Erebus Ice Tongue that sticks out into McMurdo Sound, its tip and edges sculpted by the wind into swirls of snow like whipped cream. Inside are ice caves — high neon-blue rooms of ice stalactites and giant ice crystals that rang like tiny steel drums when I tapped my fingernails against them.

Another time we traveled farther, to Granite Harbor, where I camped out on the sea ice for the first time. For four days we dived through ice cracks into magnificent sponge gardens, visited the seal pups on the ice and climbed into glacier caverns.

After our outings, I'd crawl into the tent, wrap myself in fleeces and squirrel into a thick sleeping bag set on an inflatable pad over a foam mat. I'd drift off to sleep to the sounds of seals calling to each other under the ice — an eerie but strangely comforting sound.

And in 1996, 85 years after Amundsen and Scott, I too reached the South Pole. My three-hour plane trip was nothing compared to their grueling 50-day overland trek. Once there, we visited Amundsen-Scott South Pole Station under its metal dome and the South Pole marker not far away. As I touched the marker, a chill went through me. And it wasn't just the cold. I was at 90° south — the South Pole!

This cavern in the Erebus Ice Tongue is like something from another planet. The ceiling is neon blue and the walls are coated with giant ice crystals.

I pose with my hand on the ceremonial South Pole marker, surrounded by the flags of the countries that first signed the Antarctic Treaty. This marker is stuck into a thick sheet of ice that is sliding away from the real South Pole, located about 100 m (300 ft.) away.

Farewell, Antarctica

December 1998. After seven summers diving in the Antarctic, my research was complete. While I am eager to get home to my family, I am saddened to think I might never return. But maybe the antarctic bug will grow in Janelle and Michael, my children, or affect others when they hear of my experiences.

Everywhere I looked were sights and sounds that I would remember forever. Some were small things, like the thrill of seeing the first skua of the season, the antarctic equivalent of the first robin in spring. Other memories, such as my work with sea bed creatures, had become part of my life as a scientist. But the greatest gift — and the thing I will remember most — was the privilege of going under the ice, hearing the seal calls reverberate and seeing light pour through the crystal-blue ceiling above.

I'm sitting on a rock outcropping at Castle Rock, an hour's walk from McMurdo. The view from here is breathtaking. And the air is so clear I can see for miles.

Mount Erebus glows pink and blue in the early morning October sunset.

Every day I would look out my bedroom window and see Mount Discovery dressed in a different cloud costume. Soon, I would see it for the last time.

I was packing for my flight out, but not making much progress. I gave up, and took a last climb up Ob Hill where I saw the whole of McMurdo sweeping below me, majestic Mount Discovery and the steaming volcano, Mount Erebus. It's almost unbearable to think that I might never see this view again.

I've come a long way since I first stepped onto Antarctica. I've become comfortable diving under the ice and I can stay down longer because I'm not nervously sucking up my air supply. I can float over the sea bed without kicking up sediment, and I can advise novices about how to work more efficiently and safely — just as the old hands advised me.

I've made a lot of friends here: divers, scientists, artists, politicians, electricians, pilots, journalists, cooks and mountaineers. We've worked hard, but had wonderful adventures, too — pleasure dives and trips by snowmobile and helicopter to remote areas. We've also had fun — costume parties, bowling, hockey games in bunny boots and an annual 7 km (4 mi.) run to Scott's Hut.

The U.S. Navy C–130 Hercules waits to take us back to New Zealand. The runway is ice over water. Large planes can only stay for a couple of hours — longer and their weight may deform the ice.

But my most vivid memories are of the Antarctic itself — that magnificent, frozen world full of fragile beauty.

Antarctica is the last great wilderness on Earth, a place to treasure and preserve. Our research on pollution is one step toward that goal. We found that our waste affects the animals here, and that different pollutants have different impacts. Our findings added to evidence that showed more must be done to protect the antarctic environment. It helped convince McMurdo to put in sewage treatment in 2003.

We've made a start, but there's a lot of work to do. We have to agree on how much and in what way the Antarctic should be visited, and what we should do to protect it. Many countries are concerned and meet to discuss solutions. I'm proud to be one of Canada's representatives. So, while I am leaving Antarctica today, I will continue to be connected to this amazing continent.

I step into the same bus that first brought me to McMurdo such a short time ago, and we roll over the sea ice to the waiting airplane. Our driver is talking about Christmas, and whether a plane-load of presents grounded in Christchurch will make it in time. To her, the sea ice is simply a road to the airplanes that bring people and supplies. But the sea ice means something very different to me. It is a ceiling to an underwater world teeming with marine life. I keep my eyes on Mount Discovery, but my thoughts turn longingly to that hidden world below me, under the ice.

An observation tube hangs down from the ceiling of ice, linking two worlds, Antarctica above and below the ice. Divers lucky enough to experience this amazing place never forget it.

Postscript

Since writing this book, Kathy Conlan has visited Antarctica as part of the education team with Students on Ice, an organization that enables teenagers to experience the Antarctic and Arctic. She will also return to McMurdo Station for three more antarctic summers to find out how the marine life responds to sewage treatment.

●●●●●●●●●

Photo credits

Every reasonable effort has been made to trace ownership of and give accurate credit to copyrighted material. Information that would enable the publisher to correct any discrepancies in future editions would be appreciated.

title page: Dr. Hunter Lenihan, University of California, Santa Barbara; **p. 4:** Dan Bockus; **p. 6:** photographer unknown; **p. 8:** both, Dr. Lloyd M. Hampson; **p. 9:** top, Dr. Lloyd M. Hampson; **p. 9:** bottom, Glenn Conlan; **p. 10:** Dr. Rikk Kvitek, California State University, Monterey Bay; **p. 11:** bottom, Steve Blasco, Geological Survey of Canada; **p. 18:** Sarah Krall, Raytheon Polar Services Company (RPSC); **p. 19:** bottom, Dr. Hunter Lenihan, University of California, Santa Barbara; **p. 25:** left, photographer unknown; **p. 26:** Rob Robbins, RPSC; **p. 27:** both, Jeffrey Bozanic; **p. 34:** bottom, Rob Robbins, RPSC; **p. 35:** top, Rob Robbins, RPSC; **p. 35:** bottom, Gregg Leibert, Petroleum Helicopters Incorporated; **p. 39:** Gregg Leibert, Petroleum Helicopters Incorporated; **p. 44:** Juan Laden; **p. 45:** top Gregg Leibert, Petroleum Helicopters Incorporated; **p. 48:** both Dr. Gordon McFeters, Montana State University; **p. 51:** right Diane Edwards, Montana State University; **p. 52:** top Gregg Leibert, Petroleum Helicopters Incorporated. All other photos by Kathy Conlan © Canadian Museum of Nature.

Acknowledgments

So many have left an imprint on my life. My parents, Jean and Lloyd Hampson, gave me the foundation, and my father was the first to suggest that I visit Antarctica (I responded with incredulity!). My sisters, Janet and Wendy, were my closest friends as I grew up (and still are). Derek Ellis, University of Victoria, gave me the training and the first experience of working from ships (including my one and only time in a submersible). Ed Bousfield gave me my first position at the Canadian Museum of Nature, and Chuck Gruchy made it possible for me to return to university for a doctoral degree. There, Henry Howden and Stewart Peck, Carleton University, and John McNeill, University of Ottawa, increased the rigor of my scientific thought. Peter Slattery introduced me to the Moss Landing gang and invited me to join them for my first diving trip in Alaska. Having only known me for a week, John Oliver invited me to Antarctica, suggested an Arctic program, and told me to "think big." The talents of Rikk Kvitek, Hunter Lenihan and Stacy Kim of Moss Landing Marine Laboratories, and Steve Blasco, Geological Survey of Canada, were key to making that a reality. Susan Laurie-Bourque and Caroly Ramsay have been friends to laugh with when work got overwhelming. Recently, Geoff Green and Angela Holmes of Students on Ice have introduced me to a new way of seeing the polar world through the eyes of the young. Over my 22 years at the Canadian Museum of Nature, Ed Hendrycks has listened to me exclaim and complain, and has been my dive, research and teaching buddy throughout.

My expeditions would not have been possible without the generous support of the Polar Continental Shelf Project and the National Science Foundation. The support staff at Resolute Bay and McMurdo Station went out of their way to help us and I gained many friends through working there. I am grateful to the people of Nunavut for allowing us to work on their land and especially thank the Kalluk family of Resolute Bay. The many students at Moss Landing Marine Labs and the Canadian Museum of Nature gave their energy and hard work and filled our field trips with fun and camaraderie. The Canadian Committee for Antarctic Research has given me the opportunity to link with polar scientists internationally. Most of all, I am indebted to my colleagues and friends at the Canadian Museum of Nature, who have supported and promoted me, especially Dory Cameron, who initiated this book with Kids Can Press. I am grateful to writers Louise Dickson and Iain Hunter, editors Valerie Wyatt and Charis Wahl, and designer Julia Naimska, who brought this book from dream to reality. In particular, Valerie Wyatt patiently helped me work through its many revisions.

Through it all, my husband, Glenn, and my children, Janelle and Michael, have endured and encouraged. To all of you I dedicate this book and give my heartfelt thanks.